# PRINCEWILL LAGANG

# Love Across Generations: Advice from Couples Who've Lasted

*First published by PRINCEWILL LAGANG 2023*

*Copyright © 2023 by Princewill Lagang*

*All rights reserved. No part of this publication may be reproduced, stored or transmitted in any form or by any means, electronic, mechanical, photocopying, recording, scanning, or otherwise without written permission from the publisher. It is illegal to copy this book, post it to a website, or distribute it by any other means without permission.*

*Princewill Lagang asserts the moral right to be identified as the author of this work.*

*First edition*

*This book was professionally typeset on Reedsy.
Find out more at reedsy.com*

# Contents

| | | |
|---|---|---|
| 1 | Introduction | 1 |
| 2 | The Wisdom of Time | 3 |
| 3 | Communication Through the Years | 5 |
| 4 | Navigating Life's Challenges Together | 7 |
| 5 | The Changing Dynamics of Intimacy | 9 |
| 6 | Keeping the Spark Alive | 11 |
| 7 | Balancing Individuality and Togetherness | 13 |
| 8 | Passing Down Values and Traditions | 15 |
| 9 | Growing Together: Lessons in Compromise | 17 |
| 10 | Sustaining Friendship and Laughter | 19 |
| 11 | Reflections on Lifelong Love | 21 |
| 12 | Passing on the Wisdom | 23 |

# 1

# Introduction

In a world characterized by rapid change and fleeting connections, the enduring bonds shared by couples who have weathered the storms of time hold a profound significance. This book embarks on a journey into the lives of these remarkable couples, delving into the rich tapestry of their experiences to extract invaluable pearls of wisdom that have sustained their relationships over the years.

At its heart, this book centers on the theme of collecting wisdom from couples who have stood the test of time. In a society often preoccupied with novelty and instant gratification, the stories and insights from these enduring partnerships offer a refreshing counterpoint. These couples serve as living testaments to the power of commitment, communication, and resilience in cultivating relationships that flourish over decades.

The value of learning from such couples cannot be overstated. Their stories encapsulate a reservoir of experiences that provide insights into the complexities and nuances of building and maintaining strong, lasting relationships. The lessons that emerge from their shared journeys serve as beacons of guidance for those seeking to forge connections that withstand the challenges of modern life.

By peering into the lives of these couples, we gain access to a treasury of practical advice, heartfelt anecdotes, and time-tested strategies for navigating the ups and downs that every relationship encounters. Their stories remind us that enduring love is not a matter of luck, but a result of conscious effort, mutual respect, and unwavering dedication.

In the chapters that follow, we will embark on an exploration of the various dimensions that contribute to the longevity of these relationships. We will delve into the intricate dance of communication, the art of compromise, the significance of shared values, and the role of intimacy. Through these narratives, we hope to glean insights that can be applied to our own lives, whether we are starting new relationships or seeking to fortify existing ones.

As we embark on this journey, let us keep in mind the profound wisdom that can be found in the stories of couples who have held onto each other through the passage of time. Their experiences remind us that enduring love is not an unattainable ideal, but a living reality that can be cultivated through intention, effort, and a willingness to learn from those who have walked the path before us.

# 2

# The Wisdom of Time

In the pursuit of understanding enduring relationships, we are often drawn to the stories of couples who have braved the trials and tribulations that time inevitably brings. These couples possess a reservoir of insights that can only be acquired through the passage of years, an accumulation of experiences that enrich their understanding of love, partnership, and the intricate dynamics that bind them together.

As we listen to the narratives of these couples, a distinct pattern emerges – one that reveals the profound impact of time on the nature of their relationships. The challenges they have faced, the joys they have shared, and the storms they have weathered have contributed to a depth of understanding that is unparalleled. It is within this crucible of experience that the raw materials of enduring love are refined.

The unique insights offered by couples who have traversed decades together are a testament to the transformative potential of time. While the initial stages of a relationship may be characterized by infatuation and excitement, the passing years introduce us to the realities of life – the inevitability of change, the complexities of personal growth, and the necessity of navigating unforeseen obstacles.

It is through these lived experiences that enduring couples have cultivated a wealth of wisdom. Their stories are not just tales of longevity, but narratives of resilience, adaptation, and a willingness to learn. The conflicts they've resolved, the compromises they've made, and the shared dreams they've pursued have all contributed to a tapestry of knowledge that informs their interactions and decisions.

One of the most significant roles that accumulated experiences play in lasting love is the ability to provide context. Couples who have journeyed together can draw upon a rich history of shared memories – a repository of both triumphs and setbacks. This historical backdrop enables them to view present challenges with a sense of perspective, understanding that difficulties are often transient and that the essence of their bond goes beyond momentary struggles.

Furthermore, the lessons learned from the trials of the past serve as guiding lights for navigating the uncertainties of the future. The mistakes made and the lessons gleaned become touchstones that inform their choices, steering them away from pitfalls that might otherwise jeopardize their connection.

In conclusion, the wisdom of time is a profound aspect of enduring relationships. The insights gained from years of shared experiences hold immeasurable value, offering a roadmap for others embarking on the journey of love. The stories of these couples remind us that love is not immune to challenges, but rather it thrives when nurtured by the lessons and growth that only time can provide. As we continue to explore the dimensions of lasting relationships, let us embrace the wisdom that emerges from the passage of time and the resilient hearts of those who have embraced it.

# 3

# Communication Through the Years

Communication stands as the cornerstone of any successful relationship, evolving in profound ways as couples journey through the years together. As we delve into the dynamics of enduring relationships, we discover that effective communication isn't a static skill, but a dynamic process that adapts to the changing landscapes of life.

In the early stages of a relationship, communication often revolves around discovery and novelty. Partners eagerly share their stories, dreams, and aspirations, forming a foundation of understanding. As time progresses, the nature of communication deepens, encompassing shared experiences, joys, and the inevitable challenges that life presents.

Couples who have sustained lasting relationships emphasize the importance of open and honest communication. This entails not only sharing joys and accomplishments but also discussing fears, insecurities, and concerns. This vulnerability fosters a sense of emotional intimacy that weathers the storms of life.

As couples enter different life stages, communication takes on new dimensions. During the whirlwind of raising a family, effective communication becomes essential in coordinating responsibilities, nurturing children, and maintaining a strong partnership amidst the demands of parenthood. Clear and respectful dialogue ensures that both partners' needs are acknowledged and met, preventing resentments from festering.

Later in life, as children leave the nest and retirement approaches, couples are presented with a unique opportunity to rediscover each other. Communication during this phase involves rekindling shared interests and hobbies, reevaluating goals, and providing mutual support as physical changes and health considerations arise.

Maintaining effective communication throughout these stages requires ongoing effort. Couples stress the importance of active listening – not just hearing words, but truly comprehending the emotions and intentions behind them. They also highlight the value of empathy, putting oneself in the other's shoes to better understand their perspective.

Another vital aspect of communication through the years is adaptability. As partners grow and change, their communication styles may evolve. Couples who have succeeded in enduring relationships have learned to embrace these changes, adjusting their communication patterns to accommodate each other's evolving needs and preferences.

Ultimately, the couples who have stood the test of time remind us that communication is a skill that demands cultivation. It's a journey of continuous learning, requiring patience, humility, and a willingness to listen, understand, and express oneself effectively. By nurturing a dialogue that evolves alongside their journey, enduring couples build a foundation of understanding that allows their love to flourish, decade after decade.

# 4

# Navigating Life's Challenges Together

The journey of love is not without its challenges, and enduring couples understand this truth intimately. As we delve into the lives of those who have weathered life's storms side by side, we uncover a wealth of insights into how these couples navigate adversity, demonstrating remarkable resilience, effective problem-solving, and unwavering mutual support.

Resilience emerges as a defining trait of enduring couples. The challenges they face span a spectrum – from financial hardships to health crises, from personal losses to external pressures. Through it all, these couples exhibit a tenacity that springs from a shared commitment to weathering difficulties as a united front. Resilience in enduring relationships involves acknowledging the pain while maintaining hope, and choosing to face challenges together, drawing strength from each other.

Problem-solving is another critical skill that these couples hone over the years. They emphasize the importance of addressing issues as a team, rather than letting them fester. Problem-solving in enduring relationships requires effective communication, a willingness to compromise, and a focus on finding solutions rather than assigning blame. Couples who stand the test of time understand that differences will arise, but it's how these differences are addressed that defines the health of the relationship.

Mutual support is a cornerstone of navigating challenges together. Enduring couples provide one another with a steady pillar of emotional and practical support. They prioritize being each other's biggest cheerleader, offering encouragement, empathy, and reassurance during tough times. This support goes beyond merely being present – it involves actively seeking ways to alleviate each other's burdens and create an environment of safety and trust.

Enduring couples also recognize that self-care plays a role in their ability to face challenges together. They understand that taking care of their individual well-being contributes to the strength of the partnership. This self-awareness prevents burnout and allows each partner to show up fully in the relationship, ready to provide the necessary support.

The stories of these couples remind us that the journey of love is not exempt from adversity. However, the way challenges are handled can either strengthen or strain a relationship. By cultivating resilience, honing problem-solving skills, and offering unwavering mutual support, enduring couples create a foundation that allows them to weather life's challenges while keeping their bond intact. As we continue our exploration, let us draw inspiration from their experiences, learning to face challenges with the same grace and unity that define these remarkable relationships.

# 5

# The Changing Dynamics of Intimacy

Intimacy, in all its facets, is a deeply transformative force in any relationship. Enduring couples provide us with a nuanced understanding of how intimacy evolves over time, encompassing physical, emotional, and spiritual dimensions. As we unravel the layers of intimacy within these relationships, we discover a profound journey of connection that deepens with each passing year.

Physical intimacy, a cornerstone of early relationships, takes on new dimensions as couples traverse the years together. While the passionate sparks of infatuation may ebb, a more profound connection often emerges – one that is built on trust, comfort, and a shared history. Physical intimacy becomes a celebration of familiarity, a means of expressing love and appreciation for the journey they've shared. As bodies change with age, these couples emphasize the importance of open communication about desires and concerns, fostering an environment of acceptance and understanding.

Emotional intimacy evolves in tandem with the growth of enduring relationships. Partners learn to share their vulnerabilities, fears, and dreams, fostering a deep sense of trust. As couples face life's challenges, the emotional bond strengthens, enabling them to weather storms with unwavering support. These couples prioritize active listening, empathy, and open communication to nurture emotional intimacy, ensuring that the emotional connection remains a cornerstone of their journey.

Spiritual intimacy, often overlooked, is a vital dimension that endures couples explore. This doesn't necessarily refer to religious beliefs, but rather a shared sense of purpose, values, and connection to something greater than themselves. Over the years, couples discover a sense of unity in their life's mission and values, cultivating a sense of spiritual intimacy that binds them even closer together.

As relationships mature, the dynamic interplay between these dimensions of intimacy becomes more intricate. Partners learn to balance the ebb and flow of passion, the intricacies of emotional expression, and the deep resonance of shared values. This evolving dance creates a canvas of intimacy that is unique to each relationship, a testament to the transformative power of time and shared experience.

While the flames of infatuation may subside, the fires of enduring love burn even brighter. Intimacy, in its multifaceted forms, is a journey that unfolds over decades, revealing new layers of connection and depth. As we continue to explore the narratives of these remarkable couples, let us be inspired to cultivate intimacy in all its dimensions – physical, emotional, and spiritual – allowing our relationships to thrive and endure through the changing tides of time.

# 6

# Keeping the Spark Alive

In enduring relationships, the flame of passion doesn't merely flicker; it evolves into a steady, warm glow that infuses every interaction. As we delve into the lives of couples who have maintained vibrant connections over time, we uncover a treasure trove of strategies that keep the spark of their love alive. From small, everyday gestures to deliberate acts of romance, these couples offer insights into how to nurture excitement and keep relationships vibrant.

One of the key strategies these couples employ is the art of continuous discovery. They understand that individuals evolve, and as such, so do their interests, dreams, and desires. By actively engaging in each other's evolving worlds, they create opportunities for new conversations, shared activities, and mutual growth. This curiosity about each other's lives breathes fresh air into the relationship, ensuring that it remains dynamic and engaging.

Surprise and spontaneity play pivotal roles in maintaining excitement. These couples emphasize the importance of occasionally breaking routine, whether it's through surprise date nights, unexpected gifts, or spontaneous getaways. These gestures inject an element of unpredictability into the relationship, rekindling the sense of thrill that often characterizes early romance.

Communication takes on a new dimension when it comes to reigniting the flame. Couples are deliberate about expressing their love and appreciation, even amidst the familiarity of long-term companionship. They understand that words hold the power to uplift, inspire, and renew the connection. Regularly affirming their feelings helps keep the romantic fires burning.

Shared experiences also contribute to the vibrancy of enduring relationships. Couples who have stood the test of time often have a repertoire of cherished memories that they continuously add to. They prioritize spending quality time together, whether it's through travel, hobbies, or simply enjoying each other's company. These shared moments create a reservoir of positivity that fuels the relationship's energy.

Maintaining a sense of individuality within the relationship is another cornerstone of keeping the spark alive. These couples understand that while they share a life together, they are still two distinct individuals. They encourage each other's passions and pursuits, recognizing that personal growth contributes to the richness of their connection.

In conclusion, the journey of keeping the spark alive is a deliberate one. It involves a combination of curiosity, spontaneity, communication, shared experiences, and individual growth. The strategies these couples employ demonstrate that enduring love isn't passive; it requires active nurturing and a commitment to infusing the relationship with the same excitement and passion that drew them together in the first place. As we seek to emulate their success, let us remember that the spark of love can endure and thrive, even as the years go by.

# 7

# Balancing Individuality and Togetherness

The dance between individuality and togetherness is a delicate yet pivotal aspect of enduring relationships. Couples who have stood the test of time have mastered the art of nurturing their own growth while preserving the strong bond that unites them. As we explore this intricate balance, we gain insights into how these couples have found harmony between independence and unity.

One of the cornerstones of this balance is mutual support for individual growth. Enduring couples understand that personal development is essential for a fulfilling life. They encourage each other's pursuits, whether they involve career aspirations, hobbies, or personal interests. This support not only strengthens the individual but also adds new dimensions to the relationship, as partners share their learnings and passions.

Effective communication plays a crucial role in this delicate equilibrium. These couples emphasize the importance of discussing individual needs, goals, and desires openly and honestly. By being transparent about their aspirations, they can align their individual growth with the shared vision they have for their relationship. This prevents resentment and misunderstandings and fosters an environment of mutual understanding.

Respecting boundaries is another fundamental aspect. Enduring couples acknowledge that while they are a unit, they are also separate individuals with distinct boundaries and needs. Respecting each other's personal space and recognizing when some activities are meant to be pursued alone are essential components of this balance.

Quality time is a powerful tool for maintaining equilibrium. While individual growth is crucial, spending time together solidifies the bond. These couples are intentional about carving out moments for shared experiences. They understand that these interactions not only nurture the relationship but also offer opportunities for connection and mutual understanding.

Forging a balance between individuality and togetherness requires a willingness to evolve. As life stages change, so do individual needs and the relationship's dynamics. Couples who have sustained lasting partnerships adapt to these changes, reevaluating their priorities and finding new ways to honor both their personal journeys and their shared commitment.

In conclusion, the art of balancing individuality and togetherness is a continuous process that requires conscious effort and communication. Enduring couples demonstrate that this balance isn't a tightrope to walk but a dynamic dance that enriches both partners' lives. By nurturing individual growth while preserving a strong partnership, these couples have unlocked a key to lasting love – a bond that thrives on the strength of both unity and individuality.

# 8

# Passing Down Values and Traditions

Enduring relationships are not just a journey shared between two individuals; they are also a tapestry of values, traditions, and experiences that weave through generations. Couples who have stood the test of time understand the significance of passing down their wisdom, values, and cherished traditions to the next generation. In this chapter, we delve into the ways these couples foster a legacy that transcends their own lifetimes.

Shared values are the bedrock upon which enduring relationships are built, and they form a guiding light for couples seeking to pass on their legacy. These couples recognize that the values they hold dear – such as honesty, respect, and empathy – are not only the cornerstones of their own bond but also the seeds of a strong legacy. By embodying these values in their interactions and decisions, they set an example that their children and grandchildren can emulate.

Traditions play a significant role in preserving the essence of enduring relationships. Couples who have navigated the years together often establish rituals that are unique to their partnership – whether it's a weekly date night, an annual vacation, or simple daily habits. These rituals create a sense of continuity and comfort, providing a stable foundation for the family. Passing down these traditions ensures that the spirit of the relationship lives on, carrying the legacy forward.

Open communication is essential when it comes to imparting values and traditions to the next generation. These couples engage their children and grandchildren in conversations that highlight the significance of the values they hold dear. They share stories from their own journey, imparting the wisdom they've gained from their experiences. Through these conversations, they create a bridge between generations, fostering understanding and continuity.

Creating a tangible legacy involves nurturing a sense of belonging and connection within the family. Enduring couples prioritize spending quality time with their loved ones, fostering a sense of unity and shared experiences. This connection deepens the emotional bond and ensures that the legacy is not just about values and traditions but also about the relationships that carry them forward.

In conclusion, the legacy of enduring relationships extends beyond the individuals involved. It's a legacy of values, traditions, and connections that enrich the lives of future generations. By fostering shared values, establishing meaningful traditions, and nurturing open communication, these couples ensure that their love story becomes a beacon of guidance and inspiration for those who follow. As we reflect on their journeys, we're reminded of the profound impact that lasting love can have – shaping not only individual lives but also the tapestry of generations to come.

# 9

# Growing Together: Lessons in Compromise

Compromise is the mortar that holds the bricks of enduring relationships together. As we delve into the lives of couples who have sustained their partnerships over time, we uncover the art of navigating differences and finding middle ground. This chapter delves into the lessons these couples offer on the power of compromise in fostering unity and growth.

Enduring couples understand that differences are inevitable in any relationship. Whether they stem from varying perspectives, preferences, or goals, these differences are opportunities for growth rather than sources of conflict. These couples prioritize open communication, actively seeking to understand each other's viewpoints without judgment. This foundation of respect becomes the bedrock upon which compromise is built.

Flexibility is a key element in the art of compromise. These couples acknowledge that rigidity hinders progress and unity. They are willing to bend and adapt, recognizing that relationships are dynamic and require constant adjustment. They approach compromise as a collaborative effort, working together to find solutions that honor both partners' needs.

Seeking common ground becomes an essential strategy for these couples. They identify shared goals, values, and aspirations that serve as focal points for compromise. This shared foundation allows them to navigate differences with a sense of purpose, ensuring that their decisions align with the collective vision they've created.

Time is another crucial factor in the process of compromise. These couples understand that not all decisions need to be made immediately. They are patient, allowing themselves the space to reflect and discuss, ensuring that choices are made thoughtfully rather than hastily. This approach prevents knee-jerk reactions and creates an environment of thoughtful consideration.

Forgiveness and empathy play a pivotal role in the art of compromise. Couples who have sustained their relationships understand that compromise may sometimes involve letting go of certain desires or expectations. This willingness to forgive and empathize ensures that both partners feel valued and understood, even when compromises are made.

In conclusion, the lessons in compromise offered by enduring couples highlight its transformative power in building lasting relationships. Compromise isn't about giving up one's own identity, but rather about finding the balance between individual needs and the shared partnership. Through open communication, flexibility, seeking common ground, and nurturing empathy, these couples create a framework that allows their relationship to evolve and flourish. As we learn from their experiences, we're reminded that the journey of compromise is an ongoing dance that strengthens the bonds of love.

# 10

# Sustaining Friendship and Laughter

At the heart of every enduring relationship lies a deep and abiding friendship, fortified by shared laughter and cherished moments. As we explore the lives of couples who have weathered the years together, we uncover the profound role of friendship and humor in sustaining their connections. In this chapter, we delve into the ways these couples maintain their roles as each other's closest companions.

Friendship forms the bedrock upon which enduring relationships are built. These couples understand that while passion and romance are vital, the foundation of friendship provides stability, trust, and a genuine understanding of each other's core selves. Their interactions are marked by camaraderie, shared interests, and a deep sense of knowing each other's quirks and idiosyncrasies.

Laughter, often referred to as the "glue" that holds relationships together, plays a pivotal role in these enduring partnerships. These couples cultivate a lighthearted approach to life, finding humor even in challenging situations. Laughter acts as a release valve for stress, an amplifier of joy, and a reminder that even in the face of difficulties, there's a shared source of happiness.

Shared activities and interests also play a significant role in sustaining friendship. These couples actively seek out hobbies and pursuits that they can enjoy together. Whether it's cooking, traveling, or simply binge-watching their favorite shows, these shared experiences create a reservoir of memories that deepen their bond.

Communication within the context of friendship is marked by genuine curiosity and active listening. These couples prioritize learning about each other's thoughts, experiences, and emotions. This dialogue creates an atmosphere of emotional intimacy and ensures that they remain attuned to each other's evolving needs.

The ability to let loose and be one's authentic self is a hallmark of these enduring relationships. These couples embrace vulnerability, sharing their hopes, fears, and dreams openly. This level of authenticity creates a safe space where they can truly be themselves, fostering a connection that transcends societal expectations and the passage of time.

In conclusion, the sustaining power of friendship and laughter in enduring relationships cannot be overstated. These couples remind us that while romantic sparks are essential, the warmth of friendship and the lightness of laughter provide the glue that holds the partnership together. By nurturing shared interests, embracing authenticity, and finding humor even in challenging moments, these couples ensure that their relationship remains a haven of joy, camaraderie, and enduring companionship. As we learn from their experiences, we're inspired to infuse our own relationships with the same sense of friendship and laughter that defines their journeys.

# 11

# Reflections on Lifelong Love

The tapestry of enduring relationships is woven with threads of both highs and lows, creating a rich and intricate narrative that speaks to the depth of human connection. As we conclude our exploration into the lives of couples who have weathered the years together, we turn to their reflections on the journey of lifelong love. In this chapter, we delve into the lessons they've learned and the insights gained from decades of companionship.

Highs and lows are part and parcel of every enduring relationship. These couples reflect on the joyous moments that have brought them closer – from shared milestones and accomplishments to the simple pleasures of spending time together. They also acknowledge the challenges they've faced – from conflicts and disagreements to external pressures and personal losses. Their reflections emphasize the role of resilience in navigating the lows and cherishing the highs.

Communication emerges as a recurring theme in these reflections. These couples underscore the importance of open dialogue and the willingness to address differences head-on. They've learned that effective communication is not just about resolving conflicts but about fostering a deeper understanding of each other's thoughts, feelings, and aspirations.

The value of compromise and flexibility is a lesson these couples reflect upon. They share how the art of give and take has allowed their relationships to thrive even in the face of divergent viewpoints and changing circumstances. Their reflections highlight that compromise isn't about giving up, but about finding common ground that honors both partners' needs.

The passage of time has offered these couples a unique perspective on the ebb and flow of life. They reflect on the evolving nature of relationships and how love deepens with shared experiences. They emphasize that the journey of lifelong love is not linear; it's a mosaic of moments that contribute to the overall picture of their bond.

Gratitude also stands out in their reflections. These couples express gratitude for each other's presence, for the memories they've created, and for the growth they've experienced together. They've learned to appreciate both the big gestures and the small everyday kindnesses that fuel their connection.

In conclusion, the reflections on lifelong love offered by enduring couples provide a poignant insight into the essence of their journeys. These reflections are a testament to the resilience, adaptability, and unwavering commitment that define their relationships. As we contemplate their experiences, we're reminded that enduring love is not a fairy tale but a testament to the power of commitment, growth, and the enduring bonds that are forged through the passage of time.

# 12

# Passing on the Wisdom

As we draw the curtain on the journeys of enduring couples, we are left with a treasure trove of collective wisdom that spans decades of companionship. The stories, insights, and lessons shared by these couples offer a profound tapestry of love's evolution through time. In this final chapter, we reflect on the key takeaways that have emerged and encourage readers to apply this wisdom to their own relationships.

Key Takeaways:

1. Communication is Key: Effective communication forms the backbone of enduring relationships. Open dialogue, active listening, and honest expression foster understanding and nurture emotional intimacy.

2. Embrace Change: Relationships evolve as partners grow and change. Flexibility, adaptability, and a willingness to embrace each other's transformations are crucial to maintaining unity.

3. Compromise and Respect: The art of compromise and mutual respect are essential. Balancing individual needs with the shared partnership ensures

that both partners feel valued and understood.

4. Cultivate Friendship: Friendship lays the foundation for a lasting connection. Sharing interests, laughter, and everyday moments deepens the bond and sustains the relationship.

5. Nurture Intimacy: Physical, emotional, and spiritual intimacy all contribute to a well-rounded connection. Fostering these dimensions ensures that the relationship remains vibrant and meaningful.

6. Weather Challenges Together: Challenges are inevitable, but enduring couples show that resilience, problem-solving, and mutual support allow love to endure even during the toughest times.

7. Pass Down Values and Traditions: Creating a legacy involves imparting shared values and cherished traditions to future generations. These carry the essence of the relationship beyond the individuals involved.

Applying the Wisdom:

The stories of these enduring couples serve as blueprints for cultivating lasting love in a world that often prioritizes the ephemeral. The wisdom they've shared is a guidebook for navigating the complexities of relationships with grace, compassion, and intention. As readers, we are invited to reflect on our own relationships and consider how we can implement these insights:

Take Stock of Communication: Reflect on your communication patterns. Are you truly listening to your partner's thoughts and feelings? Can you express your emotions openly and honestly?

Celebrate Differences: Embrace the differences between you and your partner as opportunities for growth. Can you find common ground and compromise when viewpoints diverge?

Prioritize Quality Time: Assess how you spend time together. Are you nurturing shared experiences and laughter? Are you engaging in activities that foster friendship?

Infuse Intimacy: Reflect on the various dimensions of intimacy in your relationship. How can you foster a sense of emotional and physical closeness?

Navigate Challenges Together: Consider how you and your partner handle challenges. Are you supporting each other and finding solutions collaboratively?

Pass on Your Legacy: Think about the values and traditions you want to pass down to future generations. How can you create a legacy that reflects the love and commitment you share?

As we bid farewell to the stories of these enduring couples, let their wisdom guide us in our own pursuits of lasting love. Let us remember that the journey of companionship is a lifelong endeavor, one that thrives when nurtured by patience, effort, and the profound lessons that only time can teach. May their experiences inspire us to create our own tapestry of enduring love, enriching our lives and the lives of those who follow in our footsteps.

www.ingramcontent.com/pod-product-compliance
Lightning Source LLC
LaVergne TN
LVHW020743090526
838202LV00057BA/6210